# MAKE IT WITH
# **AIR-DRY CLAY**

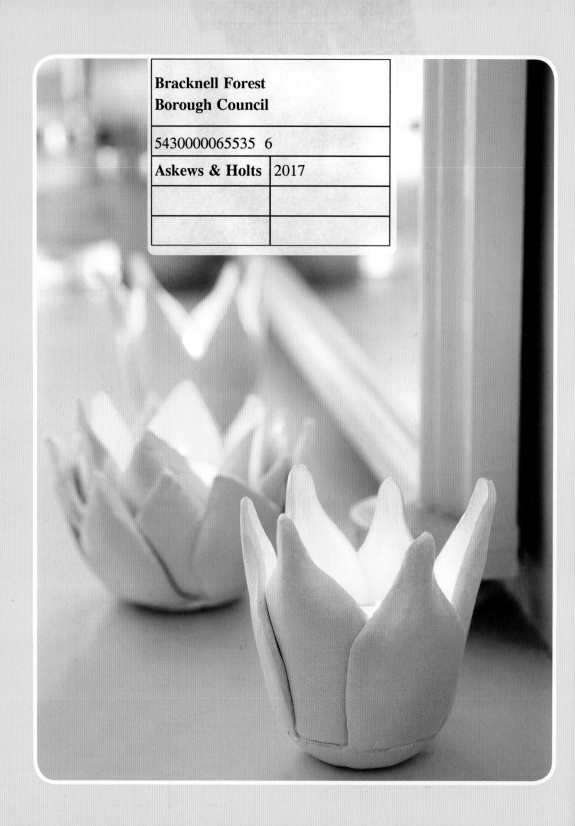

# MAKE IT WITH
# AIR-DRY CLAY

Fay De Winter

Search Press

Make It With Air-Dry Clay
A QUARTO BOOK
Copyright © 2017 Quarto Inc.

First published in 2017 by
Search Press Ltd
Wellwood
North Farm Road
Kent TN2 3DR

Conceived, designed and
produced by
Quarto Publishing ltd
The Old Brewery
6 Blundell Street
London N7 9BH
www.quartoknows.com

QUAR.ADCY

ISBN: 978-1-78221-516-5

10 9 8 7 6 5 4 3 2 1

Senior editor: Chelsea Edwards
Designer: Joanna Bettles
Photographers: Phil Wilkins
   and Simon Pask
   (project photography)
Copyeditor: Sarah Hoggett
Proofreader: Emma Hill
Indexer: Helen Snaith
Art Director: Caroline Guest
Creative Director: Moira Clinch
Publisher: Paul Carslake

Color separation in Hong Kong
   by Cypress Colours (HK) Ltd
Printed in China
   by Toppan Leefung Printing Ltd

# CONTENTS

# INTRODUCTION

I love to make and experiment with clay. My earliest memory
is, at the age of four, making a house out of clay at school
and being photographed for the local newspaper; little did I
know that I would become a ceramicist later on in life.

There are so many qualities about air-dry clay that I enjoy and
believe you will enjoy, too. To take a lump of clay and
transform it into an object is magical and, with a knowledge of
different forming and decorating techniques, you can practise
and shape it into a never-ending range of pieces. Air-dry clay
is an ideal material to use in any space without the added cost
of firing a kiln.

I could not imagine my life without clay! Once you start
making, I believe you will feel the same way, too.

Happy creating!

*Fay De Winter*

# 1

## TOOLS, MATERIALS & TECHNIQUES

# Materials

Clay is one of the most versatile materials you can use in art and design. The air-dry clay used in this book is non-toxic and also dries naturally in air, so there is no need for an expensive kiln.

## What is air-dry clay?

If you would like to create something a bit different and unique, air-dry clay is a perfect material to use. The techniques can be as simple as making a pinch pot to making a coiled vessel and using layers to build up a 3-D piece. Once your projects are dry (usually within 24 hours), you can finish them off with your favourite art markers, paints or nail polish colours.

Clay really gives everybody a chance to express their own creativity; if you can imagine something, then you can create it in clay! For this book, DAS air-drying white clay has been used. A superb introductory clay, this air-hardening modelling clay has a smooth, even, easy texture that makes it perfect for home or studio projects for artists and crafters of all ages.

Details:
• Available in white or terracotta
• 1kg (2.2lb) packs
• Acid free
• Non-toxic

## Working with air-dry clay

**SURFACES**
Clay can be modelled on any hard surface, such as a desk, using a wooden or plastic board to protect your worktop. Whatever surface you use, always clean it with water after use.

**STORAGE**
Keep clay in a sealed bag until it you need it. Once the bag has been opened, reseal it as well as possible after every use, and keep it in a cool, dark place.

**CONSISTENCY**
Clay straight out of the sealed bag will be the correct consistency to begin modelling with. However, if the clay has been kept for some time or in the wrong conditions, then check the consistency before use.

To check if the clay is the correct consistency, break off a small section and pinch it. The material should be soft enough to do so, and if pieces are torn off then they should rejoin easily when pressed together.

**WATER (SLIP)**
Water can be very useful when modelling with clay for a number of reasons. If the clay is sticking to the surface on which it is being worked, then applying a little water to the surface or to your hands can help to reduce this.

Small amounts of water can also be used to smooth the clay surface with your finger, reducing cracks in the item being made.

Brushing water onto the clay surface can produce what is known as 'slip'. This can be used like glue, to join pieces of clay together, giving a strong connection and preventing additions from cracking apart.

### DRYING

Once items have been modelled in air-dry clay, they take about 24 hours (for every 1cm [⅜in] of thickness) to dry naturally. Thicker and more solid items will take longer than this. When you are drying out pieces, dry them slowly and place a piece of plastic loosely over the top for the first 24 hours. Rotate works or place them on a dry sponge to encourage even drying and circulation of air to the piece. Only decorate pieces once they are completely dry.

Once the items have dried, they are still porous and able to absorb moisture; it is advisable to paint or seal them to give them extra strength (see pages 24–25).

### CRACKING

If you find your pieces crack during drying, you can fill the cracks with coils of damp air-dry clay (see left), but you will need to keep the plastic cover on them to slow the drying-out period and to avoid further cracking.

### CUTTING

When cutting off sections of clay from the original block, it is best to use a sharp knife. When cutting out items in rolled-out clay or modelled shapes, you can use craft or ordinary knives.

# Making your own clay

Homemade clay recipes are perfect for modelling clay projects or other clay crafts. There are lots of different recipes you can try. Do you want something quick and easy? Or would you prefer to bake your finished model for a more permanent effect? Below are two recipes that have been selected to suit these different requirements.

### MAKING CLAY WITH GLUE

This speedy recipe doesn't require much time at all, so it's great for when you just want to get going. Here's what you'll need:

- 2 cups cornflour
- 1 cup school-grade PVA glue
- Bowl

**Add the two cups of cornflour to the bowl** to begin with. This is a manageable amount to start off with.

**Slowly begin adding in the glue** Stir the mixture as you add in small amounts of glue. Continue adding glue until your mixture reaches a good consistency. The rough ratio you should work to is about two parts cornflour, one part glue.
- If it's too sticky, add more cornflour.
- If it's too crumbly, add more glue.

### USING THE CLAY

Once you're satisfied with what you've made, set it in a cool, dry place to harden.

You should only make the amount of clay needed for your project, as the clay can dry out over time, even if it is stored in a sealed container or clingfilm.

## COLD PORCELAIN CLAY

Cold porcelain clay is a great alternative to air-dry clay; it has a fine and delicate quality to it. You should note that it shrinks up slightly as it dries. Below is a list of items that you will need:

- 1 cup school-grade PVA glue
- 2 tablespoons white vinegar
- 2 tablespoons baby oil
- 1 cup cornflour
- Clingfilm
- Microwave-safe bowl
- Extra baby oil so the clay won't stick to your hands

**Begin by placing the wet ingredients in the microwave-safe bowl** This includes the glue, vinegar and baby oil. Next, stir in the cornflour until your mixture has a smooth consistency with no lumps. The texture will be gooey.

**Microwave on high for 15 seconds** Remove the bowl and stir the mixture, which will be hot and still gooey. Microwave on high for another 15 seconds. Remove the bowl and stir the mixture. The surface should have firmed up slightly.

**Microwave on high for a third time** for another 15 seconds, then remove the bowl and check the mixture. The clay should have pulled together to form a sticky, lumpy ball.

However, if the clay still appears gooey, microwave it for another 15 seconds. The end result should still be sticky and pliable; if it seems dry, you may have microwaved it for too long.

**Knead the clay** Allow the clay to cool for a few moments, oil your hands with baby oil and knead the clay for about three minutes, until the texture is smooth and stretchy. Roll it into a ball, then pull it apart to test it. The dough is ready when it stretches and forms a peak when you pull off a piece. If it breaks into bits, it's overcooked.

**Wrap it in clingfilm for storage** If you're not going to use your clay straight away, wrap the clay tightly in clingfilm to keep it workable.

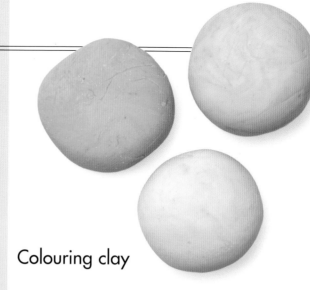

# Colouring clay

Most air-dry clay comes in plain white, but you can easily add colour at the raw stage rather than painting the dried clay. To colour it, mix small amounts of water-based paints, such as acrylic paint or poster paints, with the clay. Food-grade colourants such as cake colouring pastes or gels, but not liquids, can be used, too.

Always test a small piece of white clay first, to determine how the colour will work and to get the hue you're after.

**Knead the colour through the clay** Soften the clay first by working it in your hands, then put on plastic gloves to prevent your hands from being stained and add the colourant gradually while kneading. This will ensure that the colour is distributed evenly throughout the clay. By adding the colourant slowly, you can determine when you've added enough colour.

Work on a surface that can either be disposed of or washed easily, such as a layer of greaseproof paper over the counter top or a plastic cutting board or sheet.

If you want to make clay in several colours, separate the batch into two or more parts and colour each one separately. You can colour clay that you've made yourself in the same way.

# Tools and Equipment

A vast range of tools and objects can be used to manipulate and decorate clay items. The key is to use your imagination and try out anything that you think might work.

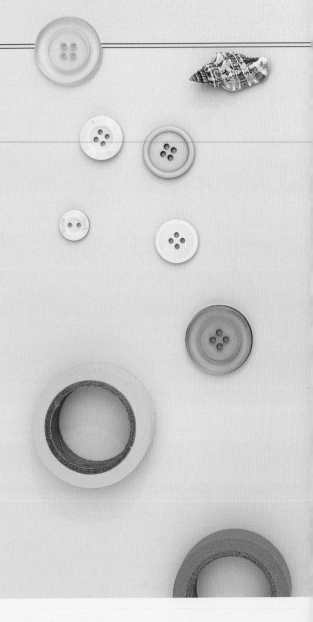

## Shaping tools

To manipulate and model the clay you will need a range of objects such as a rolling pin, boards, knives, a ruler, and different-shaped items that can be cut around and used as a template, such as bowls. When making decorative items, cake decorating cutter stamps are useful, pointed objects like pens and hole cutters are good for making sharp, neat holes through which string can be tied. Pottery tools are useful for creating surface marks and for helping with smoothing.

## Decorating tools

Any number of tools can be used to decorate the clay objects, from domestic items such as shells and buttons, to textured materials like lace and leaves. Decorative shapes, stamps, tapes, and even things like beads and rice can be pressed onto the clay as decoration.

## Paints and sealants

Once the clay piece is dry and has hardened, you can paint it. Acrylic and watercolour paints, applied with a brush or a sponge, are good for painting the clay, and spray paints can also be used to achieve designs, especially with a stencil or tape which will mask out areas.

Where possible, items should be sealed once the clay and any paint are totally dry. This will strengthen the clay and give it a better look and texture. There are a number of sealants that you can use and purchase (see pages 24–25). PVA glue is one option and one of its advantages is that it can be mixed with paints if desired to give a coloured seal.

## HEALTH AND SAFETY

There are a few guidelines that are worth noting before you start using air-dry clay.

- Keep a set of utensils specially for making clay projects.

- Be mindful of inhaling dust and fumes from clay or decorating materials such as paint. It is important that you are working in a well-ventilated room.

- Don't eat or drink in your workshop area.

- It's a good idea to wear aprons or overalls to keep your clothes clean underneath.

- All tools and surfaces should be washed down after use – mopping and washing with water is better than simply sweeping or dusting.

- Children should be supervised at all times when using cutting tools, sharp objects, paints, sealants etc.

- Always wash your hands after working with clay, as clay that dries out on the skin can cause irritation.

- Any contamination of the skin and mouth should be washed away with water immediately. If clay gets into your eyes, wash with water for 15 minutes. Seek medical advice after eye contact or if there are any ill effects.

- Don't use air-dry clay to make vessels for food and drink.

# Pinching

Pinching is a simple and easy way of forming clay into a useable shape. It is quite an instinctive process and involves creating an impression with your thumb before thinning the walls by gradually pinching them.

## YOU WILL NEED

Air-dry clay

Plastic sheet

Knife

Sponge

## TIPS AND IDEAS

- *Be careful not to pinch the pot too thin, as the form will lose strength and may collapse if the walls are weak.*

- *You can use a sponge, newspaper or an up-turned bowl to support the form while it is drying, if you find it is unable to support itself.*

- *By joining two pinch pots of equal weight and similar shape, you can make a hollow form as a base shape to develop into a myriad of different projects.*

**1** Using a knife, cut a 180-g (6-oz) piece of air-dry clay. Form it into a ball by rolling it between your hands.

**2** Dip your finger in clean water and stroke over the surface of the clay to smooth it.

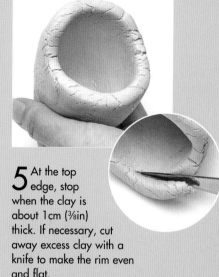

**3** Push your thumb into the middle of the ball, stopping about 1cm (⅜in) before the bottom. Begin to slowly press your thumb into the sides of the clay ball to pinch them out, rotating the ball in your hands as you do so to keep the thickness even all the way around and keeping your fingers on the outside so that you can support and feel how thick the clay is.

**4** Continue pinching the wall, gradually moving your thumb from the bottom towards the top edge inside the pot.

**5** At the top edge, stop when the clay is about 1cm (⅜in) thick. If necessary, cut away excess clay with a knife to make the rim even and flat.

**6** Flatten the top edge of the pot further by gently tapping it on a flat surface. Use a plastic sheet to prevent the clay sticking and damaging your work surface.

**7** Gently pinch the rim between your thumb and fingers to thin and even out the thickness of the edge.

**8** Dampen a sponge in clean water and smooth the surface of the pinch pot.

# Coiling

Coiled pots are constructed by stacking coils of clay and joining them together. The coils can be left visible or smoothed away, depending on the look you want. It is important to score the coils when you join them together, as this helps avoid cracking or separation during drying.

## YOU WILL NEED

Air-dry clay

Knife

Plastic sheet

Former, a cardboard tube about 8cm (3in) in diameter and 8cm (3in) high was used here

Paper

Toothbrush

Sponge

Masking tape

## TIPS AND IDEAS

- *Coil vessels can be created with a slab base (see pages 16–17) attached, to make a secure and strong foundation for the coil pot to be built upon.*

- *Remember to remove the circular former from inside the wrapped paper once the piece is finished; otherwise, as the clay dries and shrinks, it will crack.*

1 Using a knife, cut a 6-oz (180-g) piece of air-dry clay.

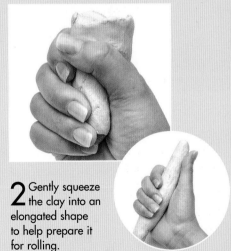

2 Gently squeeze the clay into an elongated shape to help prepare it for rolling.

**3** On a flat surface, roll the coils by hand on a plastic sheet (to protect your work surface and to stop the clay sticking), starting from the centre and working out towards the ends, rocking back and forth, spreading your hands to create an even coil.

**4** Roll the clay to the desired thickness. The thicker the coil, the more strength an object will have; the thinner the coil, the more delicate and detailed an object will become.

**5** Cover a circular former in paper using masking tape to secure it in place – this allows for easy release later on. Wrap the first coil around the base. Lightly score the surfaces that are to be joined with a knife and then drag a toothbrush dipped in clean water over the coils; this roughens the surfaces and provides a 'slip' glue that makes the joins strong and prevents cracking or the coils from coming apart.

**6** Keep adding layers. You can add up to three coils at a time before blending and smoothing. If you want the coils to show on both the inside and the outside of the pot, you need to score between each coil.

**7** When cutting a coil to fit, make sure the joins are in different places; if they are directly above one another, this may cause a weak point during construction. Dip your finger in clean water and smooth the end joins.

**8** To get a smooth surface, use your thumb to merge the coils while the clay is still soft. When merging two layers, make sure that one hand or the former is supporting the clay on the inside, while the other hand is smoothing on the outside (and vice versa).

# Creating Slabs

You can create great little sculptures or mini tiles quickly using the slabbing method. The key is to make sure you get the thickness of your slab right; if it's too thick, it will take an age to dry, but if it's too thin, your work may collapse.

## YOU WILL NEED

Air-dry clay

Knife

Plastic sheet

Rolling pin

Rolling guide sticks

Pin

## TIPS AND IDEAS

- To avoid the rolling pin leaving grain marks on the surface of the clay, rotate the clay after each rolling.

- It is also helpful to flip a slab over and roll it on both sides, rather than on just one side. In order to flip a slab, you will need two pieces of plastic, each larger than the rolled slab will be. Begin by rolling the slab on one piece of plastic. After the initial rolling, before the slab reaches the correct depth, cover it with the second piece of plastic. Spreading out your hands as much as possible to support the clay, flip the plastic-clay-plastic sandwich over. Remove the top layer of plastic (the one that used to be on the bottom) and continue rolling.

- You can create a number of slabs and join them to construct angular vessels and sculptures, such as a lidded box or a house lantern.

1 Using a knife, cut an appropriate-sized block of air-dry clay.

2 Place the clay on a plastic sheet and flatten it with a rolling pin, gradually patting from one side to the other, to help thin the clay out.

**3** Roll the clay from the centre outwards.

**4** Rotate and flip the slab as you roll, to spread the clay out in different directions.

**5** If you want to be certain that a slab is uniform in thickness, place a slat of wood of the required depth (normally 5mm ((¼in)) or 1cm ((⅜in)) on either side of the slab as rolling guide sticks.

**6** Finally, check for raised air bubbles on the surface of the clay and pop them with a pin. Roll over the surface again to make the pin marks disappear.

# Making and Pressing Sprigs

Sprig moulds provide a great way to decorate your work. Made from fossils, shells, found objects, or by carving into clay, there's no limit to the variety. You can apply press-moulded sprigs to forms, and press sprig moulds directly to stamp the surface.

## YOU WILL NEED

Air-dry clay

Knife

Plastic sheet

Rolling pin

Guide sticks

Decorative items such as fossils, shells, buttons or marbles

Brush or sponge

## TIPS AND IDEAS

- To apply a sprig decoration to a surface, put a small amount of water on the back of the sprig and apply pressure gently from the centre out towards the edges. If you are applying the sprig to a hollow form, insert one hand inside the form and press out towards the sprig from the inside so that you are applying pressure from both sides; this will stop the side of the form from caving in.

- Moulds can become wet during use and the sprig may be difficult to remove. If this happens, stop, remove the clay, and let the mould dry out before continuing.

- Ensure that whatever object you are creating your mould from does not have any undercuts. This would make it very difficult to remove your clay from the mould.

1 Following the instructions on pages 16–17, roll out about 90g (3oz) of clay to a slab about 2.5cm (1in) thick. Using a knife, roughly cut out a circular block of clay 1cm (½in) bigger than the item to be pressed. Tap the clay on a flat surface to get clean, smooth edges.

**2** Centre the object on the mould and press it into the clay.

**3** Carefully remove the object, making sure that you do not distort the impression of the object edges. Leave the mould to dry for 48 hours.

**4** To make a sprig decoration, roll a small ball of clay on the palm of your hand and press it into the now-dry mould. Press extra clay on top to fill the mould if necessary.

**5** Remove the sprig from the mould by prising it up with a knife, being careful not to damage the decoration.

**6** Using a sharp knife, trim away any excess clay from the sprig decoration.

**7** Dip a brush or sponge in clean water and smooth the edges and back of the sprig decoration.

# Surface Decoration

It is always a good idea to draw your design on a piece of paper before decorating your object; this will allow you to figure out the various stages of the design and the order in which you should apply your colours.

## Preparing the surface

Always ensure that the surface you are going to decorate is as clean as possible and is prepared according to the tips below – if in doubt give it a wipe with a clean, damp sponge, then let it dry.

## Using stencils

If you have any cutting out to do for templates or a stencil, use a craft knife with a sharp blade to ensure a clean cut and use a metal ruler to mark out straight lines. It is best to cut onto a cutting mat to avoid damaging the surface of your worktop. Be careful when cutting with a sharp knife, take your time and be patient. This is the safest approach and will result in a better design.

### ESSENTIAL TIPS FOR SURFACE DECORATION

- *You can only glue items together once they are dry, decorated and sealed.*
- *Once the items are dry you can use sharp scissors, fine sandpaper or a nail buff to help trim and smooth edges.*
- *It is important that works are completely dry before decorating.*
- *Each layer of decoration needs to be dried before adding another.*

## Brushing

You can brush and stipple colour (acrylic paint is used here) onto a surface. You may need to apply two or three coats of paint to achieve a bold, rich colour finish.

1 Apply an even coat of paint to the surface of the piece.

2 Once dry, you can apply another coat of colour or leave the brush strokes visible as part of the decoration. Sealing the work with a clear gloss spray (see page 24–25) will make the colour richer and shiny.

## Stamping

Rubber and wooden stamps are a quick way of applying simple designs to your air-dry clay pieces. You can apply them when the clay is still soft, or use them to add paint decoration to the surface once the clay piece is dry.

**1** Roll out a slab about 5mm (¼in) thick (see pages 16–17) and gently apply a textured stamp to the surface. Stamping will stretch the clay slab out of shape, so it is best to cut out the shape you want after you've stamped. Once the piece is dry, stipple paint into the stamped marks and wipe away any excess with a clean, damp sponge.

**2** Leave to dry, then seal with a clear gloss spray (see page 24).

## Masking

This technique creates sharp, clean edges and allows you to decorate without worrying about staying within the lines of your design. It can be done using washi or masking tape.

**1** Having planned the area you would like masked, stick tape onto the clean ceramic piece, making sure it is firmly stuck down, to create hard, crisp lines.

**2** Apply a thin, even coat of paint to the surface of the piece. If necessary, apply two or three coats to achieve a good coverage, allowing the layers to dry in between. When the paint is completely dry, remove the tape to reveal the uncoloured clay underneath and then seal.

## Sponging

Sponging is a great way to cover large areas quickly, while creating an interesting texture at the same time. It is a method that works well on its own; alternatively, combine it with another technique such as spattering or masking.

1 Dip a synthetic sponge in paint, dab off any excess and apply to the surface of your piece, spreading the paint out evenly. It will result in an even coat with a fine texture.

2 Here, two or three coats were applied (each layer was left to dry before applying the next) to achieve a rich, dense colour. Leave to dry, then seal.

## Spraying

Always use spray in a well-ventilated area, and wear a mask. Be aware that many spray paints are flammable and contain toxic materials. Apply light, even coats, allowing each layer to dry before you apply the next, to avoid bubbling and peeling. Use nail polish remover to wipe away any excess marks. It is advisable to wear plastic gloves and to spray works within a disposable box or on newspaper, to avoid damaging your work surface.

1 Spray light, even coats across the surface of your piece.

2 Repeat Step 1 to achieve an even coat if needed. Leave to dry, then seal with a clear gloss spray.

## Spattering

Spattering is a technique created using an old toothbrush. It can be messy, so cover your work area with newspaper or place the work in a disposable box. Wear plastic gloves and an apron to protect yourself and your clothes, too. This method creates an interesting texture.

1 Dip an old toothbrush in paint and dab excess paint off to avoid blobs of wet paint.

2 Drag your finger through the bristles to spatter small drops of paint. Leave to dry, then seal.

# Marbling with nail polish

You can create stunning abstract patterns using this technique.

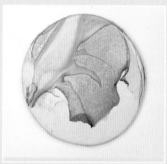

1 Fill a container with lukewarm water. Gently pour some nail polish directly onto the surface of the water, so that the colour is distributed evenly. If you hold the nail polish bottle too high above the water, the colour will sink to the bottom in lumps.

2 Slide your pre-sealed piece carefully through the water, so that the colour is evenly distributed over the surface. Let the nail polish dry for at least two hours, then seal with a clear gloss spray.

## TIPS AND IDEAS FOR DECORATING WITH NAIL POLISH

- Warm water helps the nail polish stay fluid.
- If you are not satisfied with the result, then immediately wipe off the nail polish with nail polish remover before it dries and try again.
- You can experiment with the decoration by using a toothpick to manipulate the nail polish while fluid or to spatter the nail polish onto the surface.
- All works must be sealed before and after decorating with nail polish; otherwise the nail polish will not stick to the surface and the effect may bubble.

# Impressing

There are many ways of texturing your clay. Look around your house, garden and kitchen, and you will start to see all kinds of things that can make good impressed textures.

1 Place the item you've chosen to create texture on your clay slab. Using a rolling pin, roll over it, starting from the centre and rolling out towards the edges to achieve a clear impression and sharp edges.

2 Brush or sponge paint onto the piece to create a varied surface showing the detail of the impression. Leave to dry, then seal.

# Sealing

Sealing your air-dry clay is easy and is essential if you want your piece to last for a long time. There are a variety of sealing options available and your choice will depend on the look you want and what your piece will be used for.

## Brush-on or spray-on glosses

An acrylic-based gloss is a finish used when your piece is dry in order to add a brilliant shine. All works within this book have been sealed with a clear gloss spray, but you can also opt for a matt finish if desired. Glosses work well for things such as jewellery or when you're trying to create the look of a medium such as glass. Some gloss sealers, such as varnishes, come in a thick liquid form that needs to be brushed on, while others come in a can and need to be sprayed on. You must be careful not to overdo it, as the gloss will get very sticky and leave an uneven coat. It's best to spray lightly in a sweeping motion to avoid an uneven coat.

There are also many different brands of varnishes on the market and you can find them online or at your local craft shop. A varnish is a light coat that helps with the finishing touches of your piece. It comes in semi-gloss and matt finishes. Most varnishes are not waterproof and so should mainly be used to help with the finishing touches.

## Waterproof sealers

Waterproof sealers on your project will protect it from water or heat damage. When looking for a waterproof sealer, make sure that the label says it is water-based, as that is what makes it 'waterproof'. Make sure your piece is completely dry before you seal it. Apply the sealer in a thin layer and let the piece dry before adding a second coat, otherwise you may get air bubbles or the piece may become cloudy because of the moisture that is still trying to escape from the clay.

If you apply too many coats, your piece may start to peel over time, so only apply one thin layer at a time.

1 Fill your container half full with PVA glue.

## Glue

You can use a decoupage medium such as ModPodge or Royal Coat, or thinned-down PVA (Polyvinyl acetate) glue to create a clear, but durable finish. PVA sets when there's good air circulation, and dries fastest at room temperature. Make sure your piece is completely dry before you seal it.

Apply PVA in a thin layer and let the piece dry before adding another coat. If you apply too many coats, your piece may start to peel over time, so only apply one thin layer at a time. Make sure you cover the air-dry clay piece completely with the PVA glue mixture, so there are no bare spots for moisture to get in. Brush the top and bottom of the piece separately, allowing the piece to dry between coats, so as to avoid works sticking to your worktop surface. PVA is flexible, permanent and only toxic if you eat it.

The right half of this piece has been sealed, but the left half has not. This shows how the work looks before and after applying the glue sealant.

2 Fill the other half of your container with water. Seal the container and shake well for about one minute.

3 Apply your diluted PVA in a thin layer and allow it dry before adding another layer. Two to three coats will help to seal the work completely.

# 2 PROJECTS

# Gift Box Decorations

Create customised decorations to adorn presents for family and friends or to add beautiful details to your own special boxes. Here I have chosen cutters from the kitchen, used to decorate cakes, layering them to create a lovely 3-D effect.

## YOU WILL NEED

Air-dry clay

Craft knife

Plastic sheets

Rolling pin

Rolling guide sticks

Pin

Selection of large and small decorative clay cutters

Brush

Pen

Card or thick paper for props

Spray paints (pink and green)

Masking tape

Scissors

Clear gloss spray

1 Following the instructions on pages 16–17, roll out about 60g (2oz) of clay into a slab about 5mm (¼in) thick. Push the cutter shapes into the clay, pushing down the stamps to get a detailed impression.

2 Release the clay shapes onto a plastic sheet.

3 Using a sharp craft knife, trim off any rough edges.

### TIPS AND IDEAS

- *Make sure you apply even pressure in all directions to get a detailed impression from the shape cutter.*

- *You can use a wide range of plastic or metal cutters to create different shapes and patterns, including biscuit cutters, cake decorating tools, texture mats, embossing tools and textured rolling pins.*

4 Dip a small brush in clean water and carefully brush around the edges of the cut-out shapes to smooth the clay.

5 To join the decorations together and create a 3-D effect, lightly brush a little clean water over the centre of the large flower, then place the small flower on top; the water will help the pieces adhere together.

*Fold strips of card over and insert them between the layers of petals.*

**6** Push the end of a pen (which can have interesting patterns) into the centre of the top flower to push the decorations together and help join the pieces more firmly. This also pushes the petals of the top flower upwards, enhancing the 3-D effect.

**7** Place strips of card or thick paper between the layers to help support, lift and shape the cut-out pieces. Leave the pieces to dry overnight.

## DECORATION

*Use nail scissors to cut and shape the masking tape.*

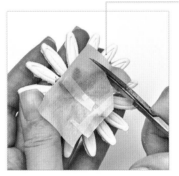

**8** Once dried, place the piece on a disposable board and cover the larger flower with masking tape. Nestle the smaller flower on top ready for spraying. Remember to spray in a well-ventilated area.

**9** Spray paint the smaller flower and allow the paint to dry before covering it with masking tape. You may need to spray more than one layer of colour, but always make sure each layer dries before applying another coat.

**10** Using another colour, spray the larger flower from above. Allow the paint to dry before sealing with gloss spray.

# Elegant Feather Tags

Create intricately detailed feathers as tags, to add your own personal messages. You can personalise them with your own colours, or brush or sponge them with gold glitter to create a stand-out decoration for a special day or person.

## YOU WILL NEED

| | | |
|---|---|---|
| 60g (2oz) of air-dry clay | Feather template on page 110 | Sponge |
| Craft knife | Card | Brush |
| Plastic sheets | Cutting mat | Ink pad (silver) |
| Rolling pin | Brush | Clear gloss spray |
| Rolling guide sticks | Hole cutter | |
| Pin | Ruler | |

1 Following the instructions on pages 16–17, roll out about 60g (2oz) of clay to a slab about 8mm (5⁄16in) thick. Trace the feather template on page 110 onto card and cut it out, using sharp scissors and a craft knife on a cutting mat. Cut out the hanging hole. Place the template on the prepared slab of clay.

2 With the template in position, roll the clay from the centre outwards to impress the shape onto the clay so that it stays in position while you cut it out.

3 Keeping the template in place, carefully cut around the outside edge of the shape with a sharp craft knife.

4 Gently squeeze and pinch the edges of the piece with your fingers to round them off and make them slightly thinner than the rest of the piece.

5 Dip a brush in clean water and gently brush over the edges of the piece to smooth out the clay.

## TIPS AND IDEAS

- When you create the hole, make sure you position it at least 5mm (¼in) away from the edge, to give the piece strength and prevent cracking.

- Make a plastic version of the template, so that you can use it over and over again. Paper and card can become damaged if used many times on damp clay.

- If the piece becomes misshapen, re-trim it.

- When applying the decoration, take care not to cut all the way through the piece.

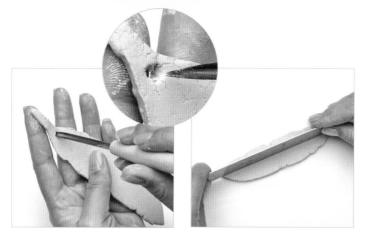

**6** Push a hole cutter through the clay near the top of the feather to create a hole so that you will be able to thread ribbon through later.

**7** Using the edge of a ruler, press a central 'vein' down the middle of the feather, taking care not to push it all the way through the clay.

**8** Using a craft knife, scratch finer lines into the clay at an angle of about 45° to the central vein to create the feather barbs, leaving the back of the piece blank so that you can write your own personal message.

**9** Use a wet brush to smooth the edges of the hole. Leave the pieces to dry overnight.

*Dampen a sponge with clean water and gently smooth the edges and back of the piece.*

**DECORATION**

**10** Gently press your dried feather into the ink pad, covering it in stages.

**11** Repeat the process until the coverage is even. Once the ink has dried, seal the piece with gloss spray (see page 24).

# Festive Hanging Decorations

Inject some festive cheer into your home with these fantastic homemade Christmas decorations. You can choose different Christmas-themed shapes such as gingerbread men, stars or snowflakes, and then add textures and colours to produce unique creations with all of the family.

## YOU WILL NEED

| | | |
|---|---|---|
| Air-dry clay | Textured material such as lace, beads or rice | Brush |
| Knife | | Acrylic paints (silver) |
| Plastic sheets | Large snowflake cutter, measuring 9 x 9cm (3½ x 3½in) | Sponge |
| Rolling pin | | Paint palette |
| Rolling guide sticks | Small decorative cutters for internal detail | Ribbon or wire for hanging |
| Pin | Hole cutter | Clear gloss spray |

1 Following the instructions on pages 16–17, roll out about 60g (2oz) of clay to a slab about 8mm (⅜in) thick. Place a piece of lace over the top and roll evenly from the centre outwards to impress the pattern of the fabric onto the clay.

*Don't cut too close to the edge of the larger shape, otherwise it will weaken the design.*

2 Using a snowflake cutter, cut out one large clay snowflake.

3 With the original cutter still in place to prevent the piece from stretching and losing its shape, use smaller cutters to cut out shapes inside the snowflake and add detail.

### TIPS AND IDEAS

- *Use different textures and decorative cutters to create a range of shapes and finishes.*
- *Impress decoration on both sides of the slab, by placing the material on both sides before rolling out.*

**4** Gently release the cut-out snowflake onto a plastic sheet.

**5** On the decorated side of the piece, push a hole cutter through the clay so that you will be able to thread ribbon or wire through later, placing it away from the edge to avoid cracking.

**6** Use a wet brush to smooth the edges. Leave the piece to dry overnight.

## DECORATION

**7** Using acrylic paint and a dry sponge, begin to dab the paint onto the snowflake.

**8** Use the paint sparingly so that the incised portions do not become flooded with paint. When you are happy with the finish, allow the paint to dry and seal with gloss spray.

*By adding the paint in small quantities, the incised pattern will remain visible.*

# Heart Wall Hanging

Hanging hearts are a simple decoration that can enhance the interior of any room, adding a subtle touch of character and romance to your home.

## YOU WILL NEED

Air-dry clay

Knife

Plastic sheets

Rolling pin

Rolling guide sticks

Pin

Small decorative stamp

Five heart-shaped cutters, ranging in size from 9 x 9cm–5 x 5cm (3½ x 3½in–2 x 2in)

Sponge

Hole cutter

Brush

Ribbon for hanging

Acrylic paint (pink)

Clear gloss spray

**1** Following the instructions on pages 16–17, roll out about 60g (2oz) of clay to a slab about 8mm (⁵⁄₁₆in) thick. Press a decorative stamp all over the surface of the slab to create pattern and texture.

*Arranging your cutters like this will maximise the number of pieces you can create from each slab.*

**2** Using heart-shaped cutters, cut out a range of hearts in different sizes.

**3** Gently release the clay shapes onto a plastic sheet.

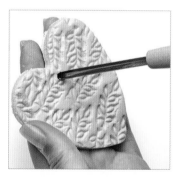

**4** On the decorated side of the pieces, push a hole cutter through the clay so that you will be able to thread ribbon or wire through later, placing it away from the edge to avoid cracking.

*Getting the depth right of the incised pattern will ensure it stands out at the decorating stage.*

## TIPS AND IDEAS

- *Do not press the stamps too hard; apply even pressure in all directions to achieve a detailed impression.*
- *This project can be customised by using different decorative stamps and creating textures using fabric, to develop your own individual themes.*

**5** Dampen a sponge in clean water and gently smooth the edges and back of the piece.

**6** Use a wet brush to smooth the edges of the holes. Leave the pieces to dry overnight.

## DECORATION

**7** Stipple acrylic paint onto the surface of the heart. Do not leave the paint to dry.

**8** Before the paint dries, wipe it off with a damp sponge. This should leave paint in the incised areas, but not on the surface of the piece.

**9** Work in stages across the heart so that the paint doesn't dry in one portion before you've sponged it back. Seal with gloss spray once dry. Repeat this process for all the heart shapes. Thread the heart shapes onto ribbon and hang.

# Impressed Trinket Dishes

Create elegant and beautiful handmade dishes with impressed textures using lace, stamps or leaves found in your own garden to give that personal touch. This project has a never-ending range of possibilities. You can experiment with different dish shapes and surface decoration techniques, made for friends or to fit your own style and home décor.

## YOU WILL NEED

Air-dry clay

Knife

Plastic sheets

Rolling pin

Rolling guide sticks

Pin

Textured fabric, such as lace, embossed wallpaper, grip mats, wool and hessian.

Bowl

Craft knife

Sponge

Aluminium foil

Watercolour paint (blue and green)

Brush

Clear gloss spray

**1** Following the instructions on pages 16–17, roll out about 60g (2oz) of clay to a slab about 1cm (⅜in) thick on a plastic sheet. Place a piece of textured fabric over the top and roll evenly from the centre outwards to impress the pattern of the fabric onto the clay.

**2** Remove the textured fabric and place a bowl upside down on the clay slab. Carefully cut around it with a craft knife.

**3** Dampen a sponge in clean water. With the cut-out clay flat on your work surface, carefully smooth the edges.

**TIPS AND IDEAS**

- *Create a range of dishes by applying different textures to the flat slab using found objects – for example, leaves from your garden – or decorative stamps.*

- *Use different sizes and shapes of bowls to create a range of dishes.*

- *Press the foil into the bowl to create a deep dish or lay it on top and slightly curve the foil to create a shallow dish.*

- *If you remove too much paint when decorating, you can add more and repeat the process.*

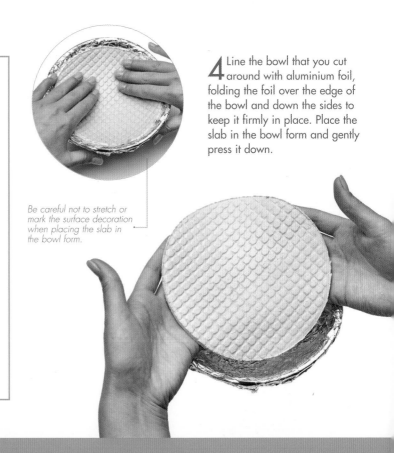

*Be careful not to stretch or mark the surface decoration when placing the slab in the bowl form.*

**4** Line the bowl that you cut around with aluminium foil, folding the foil over the edge of the bowl and down the sides to keep it firmly in place. Place the slab in the bowl form and gently press it down.

**5** Leave the pieces to dry overnight. Once dry, remove the clay dish from the bowl by using the aluminium foil to lift and release.

## DECORATION

**6** Using watercolour paint, brush areas with one colour, building up the surface decoration on the dish.

**7** Switch to another colour, and cover the areas which have not yet been painted. You can layer the colour to create more dense patches.

**8** Using a damp sponge, wipe away the paint, working from the centre out towards the edge of the piece. Make sure your sponge is only damp and not too wet, as this may flood the coloured areas.

**9** Once wiped back, creating an incised subtle decoration, leave the piece to dry. Seal with clear gloss spray once the item is dry.

*Subtle colour effects can be achieved, or you can add more layers of paint to create a bolder finish.*

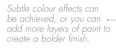

# Miniature Mirror

Creating finishing touches around your home is both personally rewarding and useful. This framed mirror will add a beautiful detail to your home, reminding you of its creation every time you see your reflection.

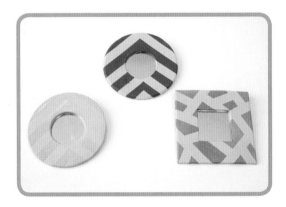

## YOU WILL NEED

Air-dry clay

Knife

Plastic sheets

Rolling pin

Rolling guide sticks

Pin

Bowl, 12cm (5in) in diameter

Cardboard tube, 5cm (2in) in diameter, with a thick rim

Circular mirror, 5cm (2in) in diameter

Brush

Sponge

Thin wire

Wire cutters

Washi tape

Spray paint (blue)

Clear gloss spray

**1** Following the instructions on pages 16–17, roll out about 60g (2oz) of clay to a slab about 1cm (⅜in) thick. Place a bowl upside down on the clay and carefully cut around it with a craft knife.

**2** Place a cardboard tube in the centre of the clay circle, press it part way through the clay, then remove.

**3** Using a knife, cut away the inner circle imprint left by the tube. This will create a recess for the mirror to sit in. Gently push the mirror into the cut-out hole.

**4** Use a wet brush to smooth the edges of the clay around the mirror on the front and back of the piece.

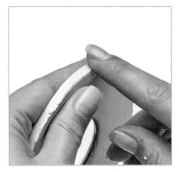

**5** Dip your finger in water and run it around the outside edge to smooth the clay.

**6** Dampen a sponge in clean water and wipe it around the outside edge to smooth it further.

**7** Cut a 6cm (2½in) length of wire for hanging the piece, bend it into a loop and twist the ends securely together, leaving a loop about 2.5cm (1in) long.

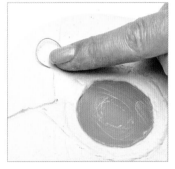

**8** On the back of the piece, push the twisted ends of the wire into the clay, leaving the loop sticking up slightly. Wet your finger and use it to smooth the clay over the wire and tidy up the back of the piece. Leave the piece to dry completely on a flat surface, face down.

## DECORATION

**9** Using washi tape, mask the mirror with a 'chevron' pattern onto the surface of the frame, folding the ends of the tape over the edge of the frame. Make sure the tape is secure.

**10** Spray paint the piece evenly. If needed, once dry, apply a second coat to give better coverage. Do not spray too thickly, as this will create drips and air bubbles on the surface.

**11** Remove the washi tape from the frame, but not from the mirror, and seal with clear gloss spray. Once dry, remove the washi tape from the mirror.

# Miniature Button Pegs

Whether it's for Christmas, a birthday or any other occasion, impress your loved ones with handmade miniature 'button' pegs to hang cards or decorate gifts. Alternatively, use your button pegs to mark your page in a favourite book.

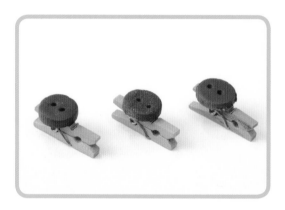

## YOU WILL NEED

Air-dry clay

Knife

Plastic sheets

Rolling pin

Rolling guide sticks

Circular cutter, 1.5cm (⅝in) in diameter

Thick needle clay tool

Brush

Twine

Superglue

Miniature pegs

Spray paint (pink)

Scissors

Clear gloss spray

**1** Following the instructions on pages 16–17, roll out about 90g (3oz) of clay to a slab about 5mm (¼in) thick. Push the circular cutter into the clay.

**2** Release the clay shape onto a plastic sheet. Repeat to create multiple buttons.

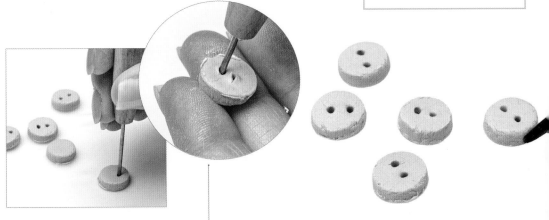

**3** Using a thick needle clay tool, make two holes on the front of each button, then turn it over and place on your hand. Re-pierce the holes from the back to the front so that you have a clean hole going all the way through.

*Support the button when re-piercing the back, but be careful not to injure yourself.*

**4** Dip a small brush in clean water and carefully brush around the edges of the buttons to smooth the clay. You can also use your finger to help smooth out uneven edges. Leave the pieces to dry overnight.

## DECORATION

**6** Once the coloured spray has dried, seal the buttons with clear gloss spray to give a shiny finish.

*Trim any rough edges with sharp scissors once the pieces are dry.*

**5** In a well-ventilated area, evenly spray the buttons from all directions to gain good surface coverage.

**7** Super-glue buttons to miniature pegs, then use the pegs to hang cards on a length of twine.

# Coral Ring

Create customised costume jewellery for every occasion, using found objects that capture those special moments and places in your life.

## YOU WILL NEED

Air-dry clay

Knife

Plastic sheet

Rolling pin

Rolling guide sticks

Pin

Brush

Sponge

Decorative item such as a small piece of coral

Adjustable ring blank with a 2cm (¾in) flat pad

Superglue

Ink pad (copper)

Clear gloss spray

**1** Following the instructions on pages 18–19, make a sprig mould of your chosen object using about 90g (3oz) of air-dry clay. I used a piece of coral for this project. Leave it to dry for 48 hours.

**2** Roll a small ball of clay in the palm of your hand and press it into the mould. Press extra clay on top to fill the mould if need be.

**3** Remove the sprig from the mould, being careful not to damage the decoration.

**4** Using a sharp knife, shape and trim any excess clay from the sprig decoration.

**5** Dip your finger in clean water and smooth the edges of the sprig decoration.

### TIPS AND IDEAS

- Decorate your sprig in colours that coordinate with your costume or outfit.

- Remember that the item you select for the sprig decoration needs to be bigger than the flat pad of the ring blank.

- If necessary, once you've decorated the sprig decoration, use a dab of superglue to attach the sprig decoration firmly to the ring blank.

6 With a damp sponge smooth the back of the sprig decoration.

7 Gently press a ring blank into the centre back of the sprig decoration.

8 Leave the piece to dry overnight on a dry sponge. This allows air to circulate and prevents the surface of the sprig from being damaged.

## DECORATION

9 Gently press the ring onto the surface of the ink pad repeatedly to create an even coat of colour.

10 If needed, apply wet ink with a brush to any areas that have not been covered. Do not touch the surface of the ring, as this will remove the ink colour.

11 Once the piece is dry, seal the surface with clear spray to create a gloss finish.

# Coloured-clay Bead Necklace

Enjoy creating a unique and contemporary necklace using a range of bead shapes, coloured clays and marbled finishes.

## YOU WILL NEED

Air-dry clay

Knife

Plastic sheet

Toothpicks

Sponge

Brush

Water container

Acrylic paints (yellow, black, white, pink and red)

Paint palette

Clay pin tool

Plastic gloves

Leather cord, 3mm (⅛in) thick and 90cm (35in) long

1 Select the palette for your beads. I have used grey and white for the marbled beads (as seen being mixed here) and yellow, pale pink and orange for the solid-coloured beads.

2 Cut seven pieces of clay, weighing about 5g (⅛oz) each. Wear clean plastic gloves when you add paint to your clay and change them after every colour to avoid contaminating the different colours.

3 Shape the coloured clay into different bead shapes, about 2cm (¾in) in diameter or length. To create a ball, roll the clay in the palm of your hand.
To produce a disc, make a ball of clay and then flatten it on a clean hard surface on both sides. A tube is made by rolling a small coil (refer to pages 14–15) and flattening the ends on a flat surface.

## TIPS

- You can make different shapes and textured beads by using one of the surface decoration techniques on pages 20–23.

- To get a really convincing marbled effect, add a little paint and twist the clay when mixing the colour in.

- Once dry, you can add a second layer of colour on the surface of the bead to ensure a really solid coat.

4 Push a clay pin tool all the way through the centre of the beads.

5 Re-pierce the hole from the other side with a toothpick to make sure it has gone all the way through.

**6** Gently rotate the bead on the toothpick, to open up the hole to about 3mm (⅛in), so that it is wide enough for your cord to fit through.

**7** Dip a sponge in clean water and, while the bead is still on the toothpick, smooth the surface of the bead with the sponge.

**8** Place the toothpick in some excess clay, to allow the piece to dry overnight.

**FINISHING**

**9** Remove the toothpick. Dip a small brush in clean water and smooth the clay around the edges of the holes.

**10** Once completely dry, string the beads in your chosen order onto the length of cord.

**11** Knot the cord ends and now your necklace is ready for you to wear!

# Bird Brooch

These cute bird brooches are the perfect project for craft beginners; they are great fun and will perch happily on your lapel all day long.

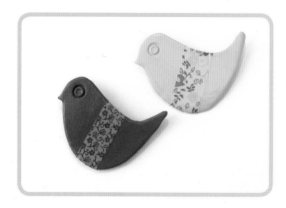

## YOU WILL NEED

| | | |
|---|---|---|
| Air-dry clay | Template on page 110 | Small, circular stamp or a pen |
| Knife | Card | Brooch back finding, 25mm (1in) in length |
| Plastic sheets | Scissors or craft knife | |
| Rolling pin | Cutting mat | Superglue |
| Rolling guide sticks | Brush | Spray paint (blue) |
| Pin | Sponge | Washi tape |

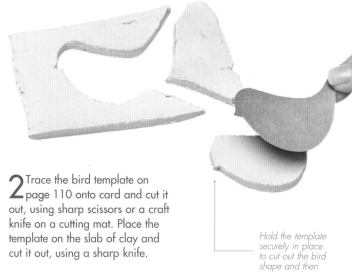

1 Following the instructions on pages 16–17, roll out about 60g (2oz) of clay to a slab about 5mm (¼in) thick.

2 Trace the bird template on page 110 onto card and cut it out, using sharp scissors or a craft knife on a cutting mat. Place the template on the slab of clay and cut it out, using a sharp knife.

*Hold the template securely in place to cut out the bird shape and then remove to finish.*

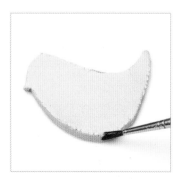

3 Dip a brush in clean water and smooth the edges of the cut-out shape.

4 Dip a sponge in clean water and smooth the front and back of the bird.

5 Apply an eye detail to the piece using a round decorative stamp or the end of a pen. Be careful not to press all the way through.

## DECORATION

**6** Leave the piece to dry overnight. In a well-ventilated area, spray an even coat of paint onto the front of the piece.

**7** Once dry, add washi tape to the front of the piece and fold the ends of the tape over the edge of the piece.

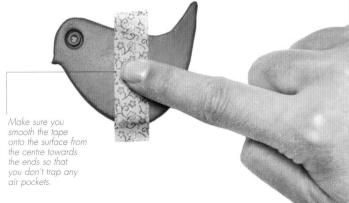

Make sure you smooth the tape onto the surface from the centre towards the ends so that you don't trap any air pockets.

## TIPS AND IDEAS

- When gluing the brooch back on, make sure that the piece is balanced when it hangs and does not tilt forwards with the weight of the piece.

- You can apply texture to the bird before cutting out the shape to add further detail.

- Why not try making your birds in all different colours or with alternative surface decorations and additions, for something a little bit different?

- Create customised pieces using your own flat templates.

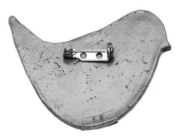

**8** Spray the back of the piece and, once dry, attach the brooch back finding using superglue to the back of the piece. Place it in the centre, 1cm (½in) from the top.

# Shell Earrings

Your outfit is not complete until you put on your favourite pair of earrings. You can either follow these steps exactly, or let our design inspire your own ideas.

## YOU WILL NEED

Air-dry clay

Knife

Plastic sheets

Rolling pin

Rolling guide sticks

Pin

Brush

Decorative item e.g. a shell

2 x flat-back stud earring posts, 6mm (¼in) across, and scroll-back findings

Superglue

Ink pad (gold)

Clear gloss spray

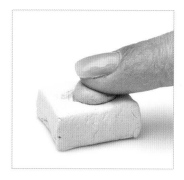

1 Following the instructions on pages 18–19, make a sprig mould of your chosen object using about 90g (3oz) of air-dry clay. I used a shell for this project. Leave it to dry for 48 hours. Roll a small ball of clay in the palm of your hand and press it into the mould. Press extra clay on top to fill the mould if necessary.

2 Use a knife to prise the sprig out of the mold, being careful not to damage the decoration.

3 Trim any excess clay from the sprig decoration with a sharp knife. Dip a brush in clean water and smooth the edges and the back of the sprig decoration.

*Your sprig mould can be used repeatedly.*

**DECORATION**

6 Once the pieces have been sealed using gloss spray, superglue a flat-back stud earring post to the centre of each piece.

4 Repeat Steps 2–3 to create a second earring. Leave the pieces to dry overnight.

5 Gently press both earrings into the gold ink. Be careful not to touch the decorated surface as you will remove the ink and may need to reapply it.

**TIPS AND IDEAS**

• *When making sprig moulds for earrings, make sure that the pieces are bigger than the flat-back parts of the earring posts.*

# Miniature Bird Sculpture

A delightful little bird sculpture to display in the home, this would make a super gift, too. Being small, it will encourage you and your friends to explore and discover other little artistic treasures that could be tucked into your shelves.

## YOU WILL NEED

Air-dry clay

Knife

Plastic sheet

Rolling pin

Rolling guide sticks

Thick needle clay tool

Brush

1.25mm (18-gauge) wire

Wire cutters

Acrylic paint (green, yellow and pink)

Clear gloss spray

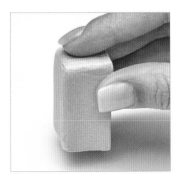

1 Following the instructions on pages 16–17, roll and cut a 90g (3oz) slab of air-dry clay, measuring 4cm (1½in) in length and 2cm (¾in) in both height and width. Tap the clay on a flat plastic sheet to help shape it and create sharp edges.

2 Smooth the edges of the block by sliding the clay on a wet plastic sheet in a circular motion.

3 Roll a small ball of clay, about 1.5cm (⅝in) in diameter, on the palm of your hands.

*Each bird you model will vary slightly in shape, thus making each one unique.*

4 Shape it into a cone shape with a rounded base by rolling it on a flat surface.

5 Manipulate the clay, gently pinching the edges to add detail, creating a tail and head. Repeat Steps 3–5 to create a second bird.

6 Dip a brush in clean water and smooth the surfaces of the birds.

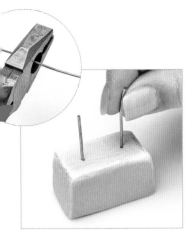

**7** Using wire cutters, cut two 3cm (1¼in) lengths of wire. Push the wires into the slab of clay that you made in Steps 1 and 2, positioning them 1cm (½in) away from the side edges and 2cm (¾in) apart.

**8** Place the birds onto the pieces of wire, being careful not to push the wire completely through the modelled additions.

**9** Using a thick needle, make a series of small holes in the bottom of the base block; this will help the piece dry evenly and avoid cracking. Leave the pieces to dry completely.

## TIPS AND IDEAS

- Be careful not to push the birds so far down the wires that the wire comes out through the top.
- Make a whole range of miniature sculptures in this way, featuring simple objects such as flowers, owls, hats or stars.
- Cut the wire at different lengths to vary the height of the pieces.
- If you do pierce through the bird or base block, reseal the holes with clay and smooth the surface with a wet brush or sponge.

## DECORATION

**10** Using acrylic paint, cover the base block evenly. You can add a second coat to get more uniform coverage.

**11** Carefully paint the birds using different colours. When the paint is dry, seal the piece with clear gloss spray.

# Miniature House Sculpture

To make small art that fits into the palm of your hand, but is big enough to have its own role as home décor, try creating miniature sculptures of houses.

## YOU WILL NEED

Air-dry clay

Knife

Plastic sheet

Rolling pin

Rolling guide sticks

Thick needle clay tool

Brush

Modelling tools

Template on page 110

Card

Scissors or craft knife

Cutting mat

Watercolour paint (orange and brown)

Clear gloss spray

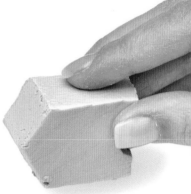

1 Following the instructions on pages 16–17, roll and cut a 90-g (3-oz) slab of air-dry clay, measuring 4.5cm (1¾in) long, 3.5cm (1⅜in) high and 2.5cm (1in) deep.

2 Trace the house template on page 110 onto card and cut it out, using sharp scissors or a craft knife on a cutting mat. Place the template on the slab of clay and cut it out, using a sharp knife.

3 Tap the clay on a flat surface to help shape it and create sharp edges.

4 Smooth the edges of the block by sliding the clay on a wet plastic sheet in a circular motion.

5 Use modelling tools to incise windows, a door and roof details into the clay.

*A rounded edge modelling tool has been used to create a contrasting roof tile detail.*

6 Dip a brush in clean water and smooth the surface.

7 Using a thick needle clay tool, make four small holes in the base of the block; this will help the piece dry evenly and avoid cracking. Leave the pieces to dry completely.

## TIPS AND IDEAS

- *Apply clay decorations to the surface, to create details such as a chimney or external stairs, for example.*
- *Adapt the size and shape of the house template to create a range of different buildings.*
- *Use different colours to suit your taste and your own home's interior.*

## DECORATION

8 Using orange watercolour, brush and cover the walls of the house. Apply two or three coats of paint, allowing the piece to dry between layers, to achieve a uniform finish.

9 Use a contrasting brown colour for the roof.

10 Apply two or three coats, allowing the piece to dry in between layers. Once completely dry, seal with clear gloss spray.

# Marbled Bead Bracelet

Learn how to make bracelets without any prior knowledge of beading. Ideal for individual and group activities, these pieces can be adapted to create a treasured keepsake or a special gift for someone to remember you by.

## YOU WILL NEED

Air-dry clay

Knife

Plastic sheet

16 x toothpicks

Sponge

Brush

Spray paint (green)

Nail polish (green, blue, pink and metallic)

Bowl

Clasp

Jump ring

Scissors

Clear gloss spray

60cm (23½in) of 0.7mm (21-gauge) clear wire

1 Cut 16 pieces of clay, weighing about 15g (½oz) each, and shape them into balls about 1cm (⅜in) in diameter by rolling them in the palm of your hand.

2 Push a toothpick all the way through the centre of each ball of clay. Re-pierce the hole from the other side to make sure it has gone through.

3 Dip a sponge in clean water. While the bead is still on the toothpick, smooth the surface of the clay with the sponge.

## TIPS AND IDEAS

- *The thick needle clay tool can create a decorative detail if pressed all the way in when piercing the bead.*

- *To create a different look, string the beads on leather cord or ribbon rather than clear beading wire.*

- *You can make different shapes and textured beads by using one of the surface decoration techniques on pages 20–23.*

4 Gently rotate the bead on the toothpick, to open up the hole to about 3mm (⅛in).

5 Remove the toothpick. Dip a brush in clean water and smooth the clay around the edges of the holes.

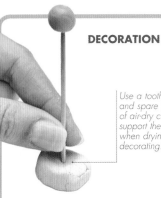

## DECORATION

*Use a toothpick and spare piece of air-dry clay to support the beads when drying and decorating.*

**6** Once the beads are completely dry, spray paint them with an even coat of colour. This will act as a seal before applying the marbling effect.

**7** Using a bowl of warm water, place and layer the nail polish colours close on the water surface.

**8** With the bead attached securely to the toothpick, dip the whole bead into the nail polish mixture and remove carefully.

**9** Once removed, use another toothpick to remove any excess nail polish that may have gathered at the bead openings. Leave to dry and then seal using a gloss spray.

**10** Thread clear wire, 60cm (24in) long, through the clasp, doubling up the wire to a length of 30cm (12in).

**11** Thread all the beads onto the wire. Depending upon your wrist size, you may need less or more beads to make it fit.

**12** Once all the beads are threaded, attach a jump ring, double-knotting it into place.

**13** Carefully trim away the excess wire with scissors

# Flower Tealight Holder

Create a beautiful floral candleholder to use indoors or outdoors on summer nights. Just one of these holders looks lovely, but a group of three gives a wonderfully subtle lit atmosphere.

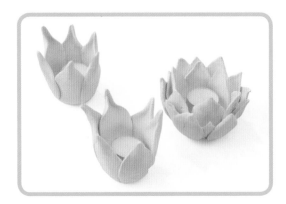

## YOU WILL NEED

Air-dry clay

Knife

Plastic sheet

Rolling pin

Rolling guide sticks

Clay pin tool

Circular cutter, approx. 5.5cm (2in) in diameter

Sponge

Petal template on page 110

Card

Scissors or craft knife

Cutting mat

Brush

Cup covered in clingfilm or a plastic bowl, approx. 8cm (3in) deep

Spray paints (white and yellow)

**1** Following the instructions on pages 16–17, roll out about 60g (2oz) of clay to a slab about 5mm (¼in) thick. Using a circular cutter, press out two base shapes.

**2** Dampen a small sponge in clean water and carefully brush around the edges of the circles to smooth the clay.

**3** Following the instructions on pages 16–17, roll out about 120g (4oz) of clay to a slab about 5mm (¼in) thick. Trace the petal template on page 110 onto a piece of card and cut it out, using sharp scissors or a craft knife on a cutting mat. Using a sharp craft knife, carefully cut out six petal shapes.

### TIPS AND IDEAS

- Experiment with different-shaped petals and surface decorations to create a collection of blooming flowers.
- If the edges of the petals begin to crack when you pinch and shape them, gently smooth them with a finger and clean water.
- Create a layered petal effect by using a bigger bowl to support the piece and making more petals to build up the decoration.

**4** Use a damp sponge and your fingers to smooth the edges of the petals.

**5** Gently pinch and bend the edges of the petals to refine the shapes.

*You can manipulate the clay pieces into unique petal shapes.*

6 Place one circular base shape in the bottom of a plastic bowl or a cup covered with clingfilm. Place three petals on top of the wet base shape, spacing them out nice and evenly.

7 Then add three more petals into the gaps between the first three already placed.

8 Once constructed, sponge and brush over the overlapping petals with clean water to smooth the joins and help the piece seal and stick together.

9 Gently press the second base shape onto the centre of the flower to hide the petal ends and create a flat space on which to position the tealight. Dampen a sponge in clean water and gently smooth the inside of the tealight holder, making sure that the second base shape is firmly stuck down. Leave the piece to dry completely.

## DECORATION

10 Using white spray paint, evenly cover and seal the whole piece. Decorate the top and base separately, applying 2–3 coats and allowing the piece to dry between layers.

11 Using another colour, lightly spray paint the base to create a dispersed mist effect.

# Geometric Planter

With its geometric angles and symmetrical form this planter is perfect for containing sculptural succulents and cacti. It will undoubtedly enhance any contemporary interior.

## YOU WILL NEED

Air-dry clay

Knife

Plastic sheet

Circular cutter, approx. 5.5cm (2in) in diameter

Ruler

Flat-edge modelling tool

Sponge

Toothbrush

Paint palette

Acrylic paint (yellow ochre and brown)

Clear gloss spray

1 Using a sharp knife and about 1kg (35oz) of clay, cut a block of clay measuring 9cm (3½in) wide, 9cm (3½in) long and 7cm (2¾in) high.

2 Cut away any excess clay with a knife and tap all sides of the block on a flat surface to tidy up and sharpen the sides.

3 Place a circular cutter in the centre of the top of the block, press it into the clay, and then remove it. Do not press the cutter all the way through.

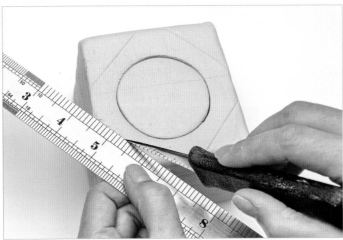

5 Measure half way down each side of the block and lightly mark a line all the way across and around.

4 Using a ruler and the tip of your knife, lightly mark a diagonal line across each corner of the top of the block, about 1cm (⅜in) away from the edge of the circle.

*These initial draft markings will help create a symmetrical and equally proportioned form.*

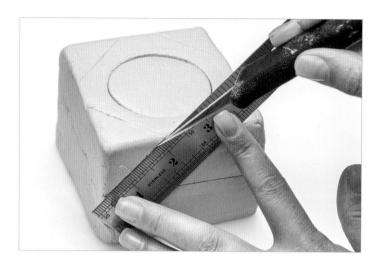

**6** From the half-way marks on the corners, mark a line up to the diagonal lines scored on the top of the block. Repeat for all four top corners.

**7** Using the marked lines as a guide, cut away a triangular-shaped wedge of clay on each top corner.

**8** Find the centre of the bottom edge of each side of the block. On each corner, cut down from the half-way mark to the centre point on the bottom edge, cutting away a triangular-shaped wedge on each side.

*Carefully cut away excess clay using the guidelines, keeping the knife steady and the angle as straight as possible.*

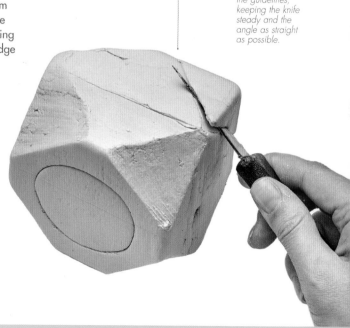

**TIPS AND IDEAS**

- *Invent different shapes and surface decorations to create a cluster of decorative geometric planters.*

- *Due to the piece being quite large, cracks can appear during drying. You can use wet air-dry clay to fill the cracks while it's still damp.*

**9** Press the circular cutter into the top of the block again and use a flat-edge modelling tool to remove the clay from within the circle to a depth of 2.5cm (1in).

**10** Use a sharp knife to cut down a further 3cm (1¼in). Remove the cutter and extract the remaining clay, using a flat-edge modelling tool and your fingers.

**11** Gently tap the clay piece on a flat surface. Lay down a plastic sheet and smooth in a circular motion with clean water to create a sharper-edged shape.

**12** Dampen a sponge in clean water and smooth the inside and outside of the planter. Leave the piece to dry completely for approximately 3–5 days.

## DECORATION

**13** Apply the acrylic paint with a sponge to the surface of the piece. You can apply colour to the base of the piece, too, once the top is dry. Dab excess paint off the sponge before applying it to the surface. Add another coat if necessary once the first has dried.

**14** Once the item is dry, use a toothbrush dipped in an alternative colour to create a fine spattered effect. Once dry, seal with a clear gloss spray. This will help the piece become impervious to water once a plant has been potted up.

**15** Once decorated and sealed, your vessel is then ready for your plant to be inserted into the opening.

# Lidded Coil Pot

Make a functional vessel to hold your precious possessions or store your favourite items. Whatever you choose to put in it, it will add a unique handmade touch to your home.

## YOU WILL NEED

Air-dry clay

Knife

Plastic sheets

Rolling pin

Rolling guide sticks

Pin clay tool

Circular cutter or bowl, 10cm (4in) in diameter

Paper

Cardboard tube, 8cm (3in) in diameter and 8cm (3in) in length

Brush

Sponge

Spray paints (pale blue, yellow and pink)

Masking tape

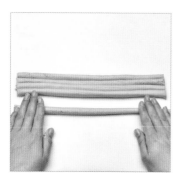

**1** Following the instructions on page 15, prepare five individual coils by hand, using 90g (3oz) of clay for each one, rolling from the centre out towards the ends to create an even coil about 1cm (½in) in diameter.

**2** Following the instructions on pages 16–17, roll out about 180g (6oz) of clay to a slab about 1cm (½in) thick.

**3** Using a circular cutter or bowl, press out two shapes to form a base and lid.

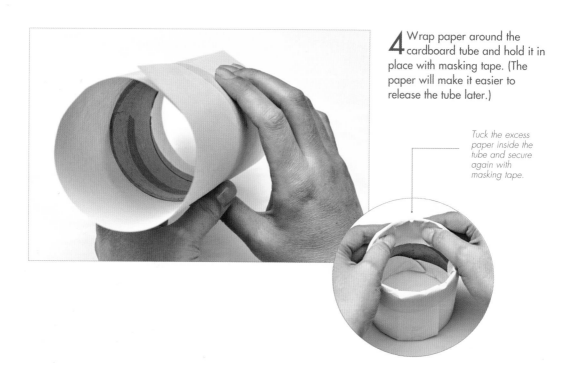

**4** Wrap paper around the cardboard tube and hold it in place with masking tape. (The paper will make it easier to release the tube later.)

*Tuck the excess paper inside the tube and secure again with masking tape.*

**5** Place the cardboard tube over the centre of the clay base, leaving about 1cm (½in) of clay around the edge.

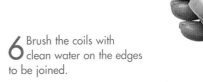

**6** Brush the coils with clean water on the edges to be joined.

**8** Using your fingers and clean water, smooth the end of the coil together.

**7** Place the first coil firmly on the base slab around the tube. Overlap the ends of the coil and cut straight through them to get an accurate fit around the tube.

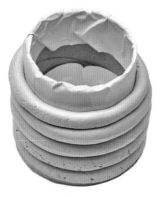

**9** Add the remaining four coils in the same way, building the vessel up to a height of about 7cm (3in).

**10** Tear away the paper and then carefully remove the tube. (If you leave it in place, the piece will shrink and crack.)

*Place work on a plastic sheet to dry and after 24 hours turn the coil pot on its rim to help the base dry evenly.*

**11** Make a small ball of clay, about 2cm (¾in) in diameter, for the knob of the lid by rolling it in your hands. Gently press it onto the centre of the wetted lid that you cut out in Step 3.

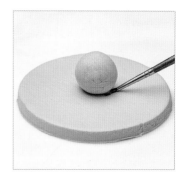

**12** Dip a brush in clean water and brush around the base of the knob to attach it to the lid.

**13** Use a damp sponge to gently smooth and tidy the surface of both the coiled pot and the slab lid.

## DECORATION

**14** Using masking tape, block out the areas you don't want sprayed. Spray paint the base and bottom coils first with the lightest colour, i.e. yellow.

**15** Once dry, remove the masking tape and re-mask over the sprayed colour and continue with the next lightest colour – in this case, pink.

**16** If preferred you can spray freehand to achieve a more gradated look.

**17** Once dry, apply the final colour, blue, to the top coil and interior of the piece.

## DECORATING THE LID

**18** Spray paint the lid with the light colour first and then mask to create a pink handle. The underside of the lid can be decorated, too, once the top is completely dry.

---

### TIPS AND IDEAS

- You can develop different surface decoration techniques by, for example, experimenting with merging sprayed colours or using masking tape to create crisp straight lines of contrasting colour.

- Create a hole in the centre of the lid and, instead of attaching a ball of clay, attach a large bead as an added decorative detail.

# Balloon Barnacles

These lovely little curio objects would make stunning tabletop centrepieces, small storage vessels, wall décor or candle holders . . . the options are endless!

## YOU WILL NEED

| | | |
|---|---|---|
| Air-dry clay | Clay pin tool | Scissors |
| Knife | Bowl, 16cm (6¼in) in diameter | Brush |
| Plastic sheets | Sponge | Acrylic paint (blue) |
| Rolling pin | Balloon | Paint palette |
| Rolling guide sticks | Clingfilm | Clear gloss spray |

**1** Following the instructions on pages 16–17, roll out about 150g (5oz) of clay to a slab about 5mm (¼in) thick. Place an upturned bowl on top and cut out a circular shape using a sharp knife.

**2** Dampen a sponge in clean water and gently smooth the surface and edges of the circle.

**3** Gently pinch the edge of the circular slab to create a thin edge.

**4** Inflate the balloon; it should be about 8cm (3in) in diameter. Put the clay slab on the round end of the balloon.

**5** Cut a piece of clingfilm, about 35cm (14in) square. Gather the clingfilm around the balloon as neatly as you can, bringing the excess clay up around the tied end of the balloon.

### TIPS AND IDEAS

- *Once decorated, use a small drop of hot glue to group several barnacles together.*
- *You can customise these in many ways: add paint or metallic effects to the insides, spray paint the whole set, or create a wall piece.*
- *Use different sized balloons to create a varying range of shaped barnacles.*

**6** Twist the clingfilm around the tied end of the balloon to create a rounded form.

**7** Gently squeeze the form to smooth out the surface.

**8** Carefully remove the clingfilm.

**9** Leave the piece to dry overnight with the balloon in place to help support it. Once the piece is dry, simply puncture the balloon to remove it.

**DECORATION**

**10** Apply 2 or 3 coats of blue acrylic paint to the inside of the piece. Allow each coat to dry before applying the next one and be careful not to mark the outside surface.

**11** Using a damp sponge, wipe away any excess paint that may have marked the outside surface. Once dry, seal with a clear gloss spray, allowing it to dry in between applying to the base and top of the piece.

# Marbled Pinch Pots

The great thing about marbling is that every bowl is different! Create beautiful unique bowls for friends and family, or just keep them for yourself to adorn your home and contain little items.

## YOU WILL NEED

Air-dry clay

Knife

Ball, about 6cm (2½in) in diameter

Plastic bag

Flat-edged modelling tool

Plastic sheet

Nail polish (green, pink, blue and metallic)

Plastic container, measuring 8 x 8cm (3¼ x 3¼in)

Clear gloss spray

White spray

1 Following the instructions on pages 12–13, form a pinch pot using about 70g (2½oz) of air-dry clay, with a wall thickness of about 6mm (¼in).

2 Cover a small ball in a plastic bag and gently press and smooth the pinch pot onto it; this will help support the piece and keep its shape.

3 Cut away excess clay with a knife to help make the rim even and flat.

## TIPS AND IDEAS

- Remember to remove the former, as the work shrinks while drying and may cause the piece to crack.

- It is very important to cover the former with a plastic bag; otherwise the work may become stuck to the former.

- It is important that works are sealed before applying the nail polish surface decoration; otherwise the effect will not stick and may peel off and bubble once sealed.

4 Flatten the rim of the bowl by patting it with the blade of a flat-edged modelling tool.

5 Gently pinch and press the rim with your fingers to thin and even it out.

**6** Gently press the bottom of the pinch pot onto a flat surface covered with a plastic sheet (to protect your work surface and to avoid sticking) to create a stable base.

**7** Gently remove the ball former from the plastic bag.

**8** Remove the plastic bag and leave the piece to dry completely before sealing with 2 to 3 coats of white spray paint.

## DECORATION

**9** Fill a plastic container with clean warm water and drop different nail polish colours onto the surface of the water.

**10** Holding the work on the inside, dip the pinch pot into the water, being careful not to allow the water to flood the inside of the piece.

**11** Remove the piece carefully and leave to dry on its rim. Once completely dry, seal with a clear gloss spray.

# Pea Pod Bowl

Pinch pots may be small, but they allow our creativity full reign. Why not create a nature-inspired pea pod bowl to adorn your interior?

## YOU WILL NEED

| | | |
|---|---|---|
| Air-dry clay | Paintbrush | Acrylic paint (red, silver and white) |
| Knife | Sponge | |
| Plastic sheet | Washi tape | Clear gloss spray |
| Toothbrush | Paint palette | |

1 Following the instructions on pages 12–13, form three pinch pots of similar size, using about 140g (5oz) of air-dry clay for each one.

2 Gently squeeze the pinch pot rims to refine them. For the two end pods, pinch out a pointed detail.

## TIPS AND IDEAS

- *Although there are exceptions, most pinched pottery is less than 15cm (6in) in diameter.*
- *As the clay is handled it dries out and may crack when pinching the edges together. You can use water to seal and smooth the cracks back together.*

3 Once you have made the pinch pots, line them up so you can work out the points where they will be attached to each other. Lightly score the edges to be joined with a knife.

4 Using a toothbrush, apply plenty of clean water to the scored areas.

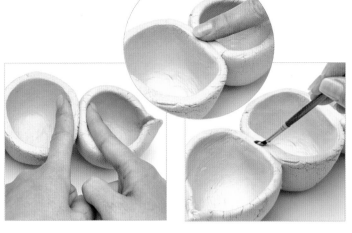

**5** Join the pinch pots by gently pressing the wet, scored edges together.

**6** Dip your finger in clean water and smooth over the seams between one pot and the next. Once the seam is completely sealed, gently pinch and stretch the pinch pots to create the desired shape.

**7** Dip a paintbrush in clean water and brush over the joins to smooth and seal them. You can smooth over the whole piece using a damp sponge.

## DECORATION

**8** Mask out areas that you want to remain unpainted using strips of washi tape.

**9** Using acrylic paint, brush different colours onto the areas not covered in washi tape. Once dry, apply another layer of paint to make the colour bold and rich.

**10** Use a damp sponge to wipe away excess paint from the rim of the piece.

**11** Once the paint is dry, remove the tape. You can use white acrylic paint to touch up areas where the paint has flooded under the tape. Once dry, seal using a clear gloss spray.

# Templates

A template is useful when you want to make several items the same size and shape. If you make them using a sturdy material such as card, you can use them a number of times.

If you have any cutting out to do for templates or a stencil, use a craft knife with a sharp blade to ensure a clean cut and a metal ruler to mark straight lines. It is best to cut onto a cutting mat, to avoid damaging your worktop surface. Be careful when cutting with a sharp knife. Take your time and be patient; this is a safer approach and it will result in a better design.

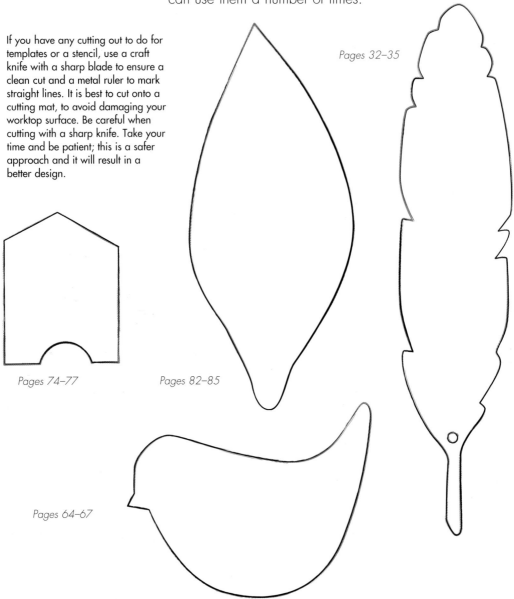

*Pages 32–35*

*Pages 74–77*

*Pages 82–85*

*Pages 64–67*

# Index

# Index

# Credits

All step-by-step and other images are the copyright of Quarto Publishing plc. While every effort has been made to credit contributors, Quarto would like to apologise should there have been any omissions or errors – and would be pleased to make the appropriate correction for future editions of the book.

Page 5: Jon Fisher (profile image); all other images by Fay De Winter.

**Author Acknowledgements**
I would like to take this opportunity to thank all those who have supported me in the production of this book, especially the team at Quarto. They have been invaluable and, without their contributions, belief and encouragement, I am sure it would not have been possible.

Special thanks must go to the people who have supported me during my studies at the University of the Arts London, Central Saint Martins, and at University for the Creative Arts, Farnham, who provided me with the knowledge and enthusiasm to develop my ceramics practice further.

I would also like to mention my colleagues at Sutton College, who were very accommodating with time and space within the ceramics studio.

And, of course, thank you to my family and friends, who were always there to support me and discuss ideas throughout the entire project. I am so grateful to have been given this opportunity and to everyone that has helped behind the scenes, thank you!